SMART GREEN CIVILIZATIONS

iNDUS VALLEY

Perfection Learning®

Indus Valley

by Benita Sen

Illustrated by Yatindra Kumar

Author: Benita Sen
Managing Author: Benita Sen
Managing Editor: Anupama Jauhry
Series Editor: Arshi Ahmad
Editor: Rupak Ghosh
Creative Head: Priyabrata Roy Chowdhury
Illustration Head: Yatindra Kumar
Colouring Artists: Neeraj Riddlan and Vijay Nipane
Image Research: Yukti Garg
Production Head: T Radhakrishnan
Prepress: Mahfooz Alam

8 9 10 11 12   PP   26 25 24 23 22

Reinforced Library Binding: ISBN 978-1-61563-812-3 or **3089902**
Softcover: ISBN 978-1-61563-806-2 or **30899**
eBook: ISBN 978-1-61384-590-5 or **30899D**

Printed in the United States of America

Contents

Teri Travels to the Ancient Past

ooouuuccccchhhh.....

OH CHOSEN ONE!

THIS DOLL BROKE THOUSANDS OF YEARS AGO. THE OTHER HALF LIES BURIED IN THE DUST OF WHICH IT WAS MADE. YOUR TASK IS TO FIND IT. THE SAUCER WILL TAKE YOU ACROSS THE AGES TO THE ANCIENT INDUS VALLEY CIVILIZATION. YOUR GUIDE, THE HIGH PRIEST OF MOHENJO DARO, WHO WAS A VERY IMPORTANT PERSON, IS WAITING.

One magical morning, Teri set off for school. Something looked different. Was it the storm that had blown things around last night? Or was she imagining things? Teri loved adventure.

As she looked up at the trees, her foot hit something. It was a toy cart, covered with dust. Something even stranger happened. "Did I just hear a soft voice telling me to clean this?" she wondered. As she rubbed some dust off, she felt a push.

swhoooooosssssssshhhhh.....

GREEN GEM The Indus Valley Civilization was one of the earliest human settlements. Its cities were well planned. The people valued cleanliness and hygiene.

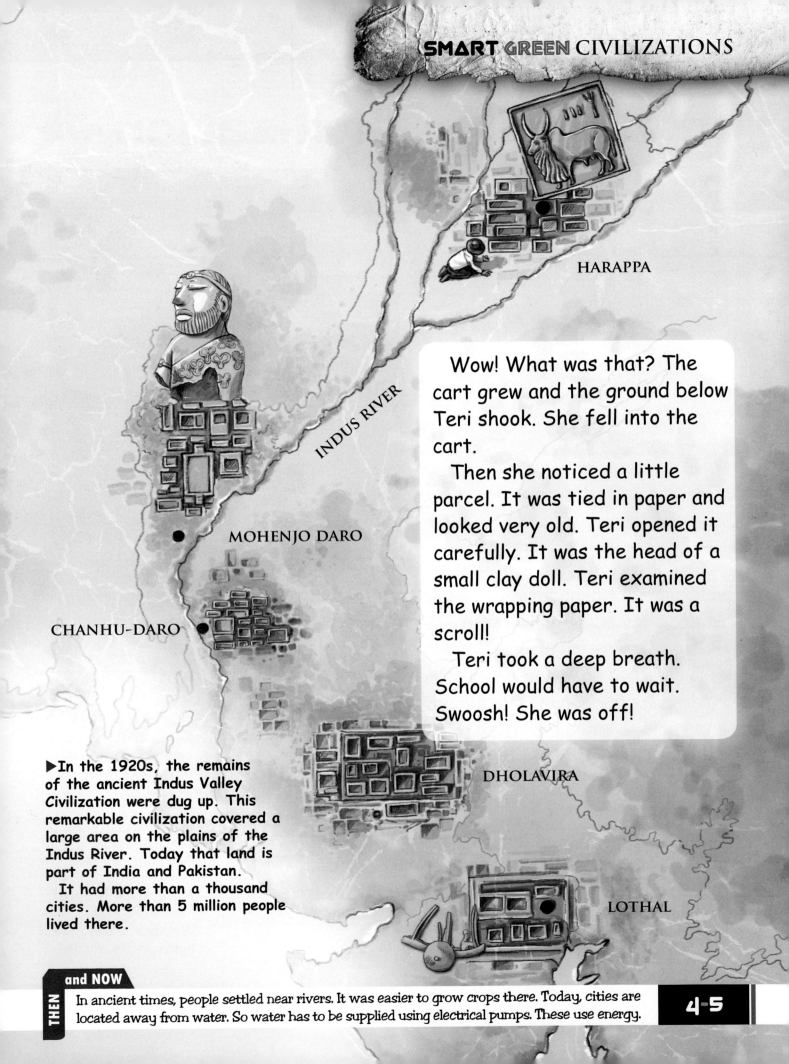

HARAPPA

INDUS RIVER

MOHENJO DARO

CHANHU-DARO

DHOLAVIRA

LOTHAL

Wow! What was that? The cart grew and the ground below Teri shook. She fell into the cart.

Then she noticed a little parcel. It was tied in paper and looked very old. Teri opened it carefully. It was the head of a small clay doll. Teri examined the wrapping paper. It was a scroll!

Teri took a deep breath. School would have to wait. Swoosh! She was off!

▶In the 1920s, the remains of the ancient Indus Valley Civilization were dug up. This remarkable civilization covered a large area on the plains of the Indus River. Today that land is part of India and Pakistan.

It had more than a thousand cities. More than 5 million people lived there.

THEN and NOW

In ancient times, people settled near rivers. It was easier to grow crops there. Today, cities are located away from water. So water has to be supplied using electrical pumps. These use energy.

Welcome to the
Indus Valley Civilization

Welcome to the Indus Valley Civilization!

You must be the Priest King of Mohenjo Daro! But what's a civilization?

Let me take you around my civilization.

A civilization is a society that is well-developed. In most ancient civilizations, people settled in one place where they could grow crops. These places became villages, towns, or cities.

The people followed a set of rules. A king or group of rulers was in charge. The people also practiced religion and spoke a language. They wrote on tablets, seals, and scrolls. They played sports, painted, and made statues and buildings.

The people of the Indus Valley Civilization built their towns and cities around the Indus River. The two largest cities were Harappa and Mohenjo Daro (both now in Pakistan). Mohenjo Daro was built between the Indus and the Ghaggar-Hakra Rivers. Harappa stood on the bank of the Ravi River.

▶The Indus is one of the longest rivers in the world. Many smaller rivers flow into it. It begins in China and flows through India and Pakistan. It covers more than 1,900 miles. This is about one-third the distance around the moon at its middle!

GREEN GEM The Indus River swells with water from monsoon rains. When the floodwaters go down, they leave behind minerals that improve the soil.

Scientists who study the remains of the past are called *archaeologists*. Modern archaeologists believe that the Indus Valley Civilization was much larger than anyone thought. It could have stretched over to Iraq in the west, Kashmir in the north, Haryana in the east, and the Godavari River in the south.

▲Harappa was the first discovered city of the Indus Valley. It began around 3300 B.C. It was large and important.

HARAPPA

MOHENJO DARO

▲Mohenjo Daro is a modern name. It means "mound of the dead." No one knows what the city was called when people lived there. It began around 2600 B.C.

THEN and NOW

Crops grew well in river valley soil. Today, farmers use chemical fertilizers to grow crops. The chemicals can harm the environment.

The Ancient Art of Trading

I can't wait to explore your civilization!

I'll be happy to take you around. See this seal here? It was made of clay about 2,000 years ago. It will tell you a lot about our life.

The Indus Valley Civilization is one of the oldest. It began about 7,000 years ago in the New Stone Age. That's when people used stone to make weapons and tools. They polished stone to make arrowheads.

Later came the Bronze Age, about 3,300 years ago. During this age, people learned to mine metals such as bronze and copper. Then they beat them into shapes. They started using metals to make tools.

The Indus Valley people traded with other ancient civilizations. They traded goods or money to get what they did not have. This made them among the earliest traders.

▼The people of the Indus Valley used metals like bronze and copper to make weapons. They also knew how to make mirrors.

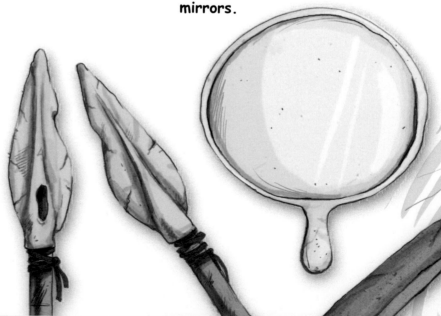

▶The people of the Indus Valley used simple tools made of wood, stone, and metal.

As far back as 2350 B.C., the Indus people were trading with the Sumerian civilization, or Mesopotamia (now in Iraq). Indus seals have been found in Mesopotamian cities. A round Iraqi seal was also found in Mohenjo Daro.

The Indus Valley seals were square or rectangular. They were made of burned earth to make them stronger. The seals were used to mark a trader's goods. They were also used to buy and sell things. Every important person wore a seal. It was strung on a cord around his neck. Seals were also used on important agreements.

Most seals had images of animals on them. This is because animals were an important part of Indus Valley life. Herdsmen kept flocks of sheep, goats, and cattle. Oxen drew carts and pulled water out of wells.

▼The Indus Valley traders used well-designed boats to carry goods across the seas.

THEN and NOW

Weapons such as the bow and arrow could not harm too many people. Modern weapons are more destructive and dangerous. Nuclear bombs can kill millions of people.

Food for All and More

The people of the Indus Valley Civilization grew most of their own crops. In winter, they grew barley and wheat. They also grew chickpeas and peas. They cooked in oil from the mustard and sesame they grew. They also grew fruits like melon, and they loved to eat dates!

In summer, their fields were full of fluffy, white cotton. They spun it into yarn. This thread was later woven into cloth.

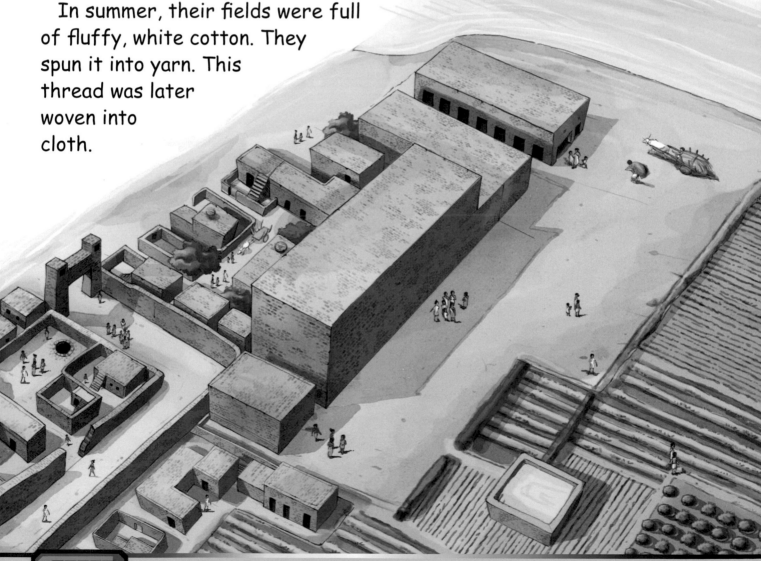

Those are fields where we grew our food.

Let's go there. Perhaps the other half of the doll is lying there!

GREEN GEM The wooden plow used the muscle power of people and animals. That's called *mechanical energy*. Today, our steel tractors are powered by fossil fuels such as diesel.

▼The Indus Valley fields produced food for all, even those who lived in the cities and did not farm. Enough food remained to sell to people of other civilizations.

Farmers prepared their fields before they sowed seeds. They used simple wooden plows to turn the earth. The water from rivers irrigated the fields.

Sometimes, the Indus River flooded its banks. The deposits left on the riverbank after the floodwaters went down made the soil rich and fertile.

The Indus Valley was a dry region. So some crops were planted in time to be watered by the rains. Rainwater was also stored in huge tanks made of rock. This water was used when there was no rain.

Farmers produced enough food to eat, store, and even trade. Fishermen also caught fish from the rivers and the sea for food.

THEN and **NOW**
The Indus Valley people were among the first organic farmers. They did not use chemicals. Some farmers today have gone back to organic farming.

10-11

Ancient Town Planners

Did you know we were the first to build our cities according to city planners?

Wow, that explains why your cities are so neat and orderly!

▶Most cities had a walled citadel. The largest is in Mohenjo Daro. Inside were the hall, a Great Bath, a granary, and the homes of the rich.

The cities of the Indus Valley were built based on plans. They had walls around them. At first, sun-dried bricks were used for homes and buildings. Later, the people learned to fire bricks and bake them. This made them stronger. Bricks were held together with mortar or paste made from mud.

Houses were built around a courtyard. That way, every room was bright and airy. The walls were strong enough to support an upper story.

Ox carts traveled on the main roads. The inner streets were too narrow for this traffic.

GREEN GEM

The Great Bath at Mohenjo Daro was the earliest public water tank in the world.

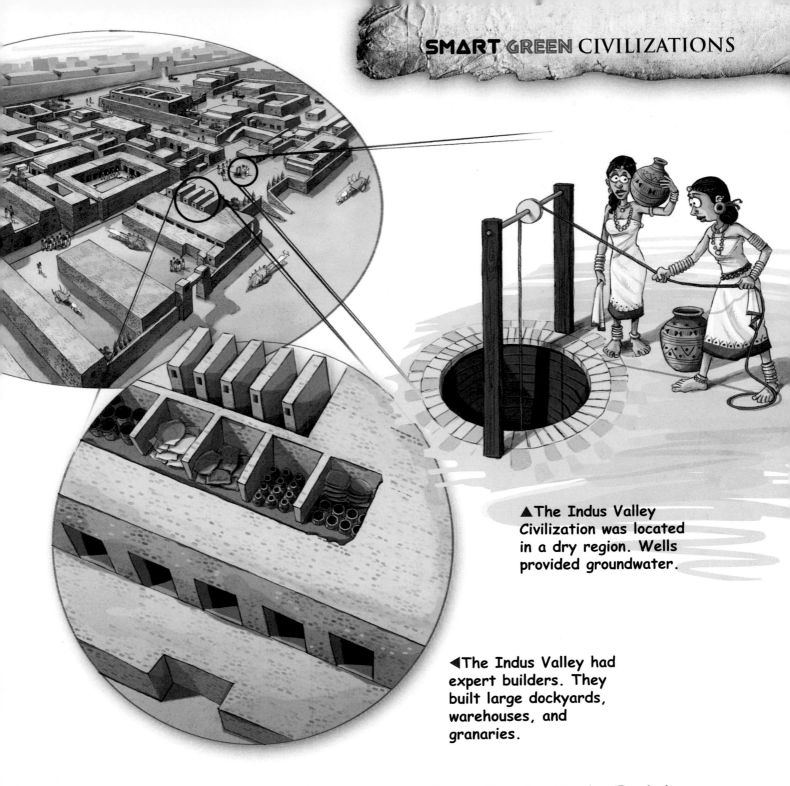

▲The Indus Valley Civilization was located in a dry region. Wells provided groundwater.

◄The Indus Valley had expert builders. They built large dockyards, warehouses, and granaries.

Large public houses served as meeting places for festivals. Each house had many rooms. The roof was held up by wooden logs.

Water came from wells. Mohenjo Daro had about 700. Many homes had their own wells. Others drew water from common wells.

Each block of houses had at least one well. These common wells were dug on roadsides. This ensured that people did not have to go far for water.

THEN and NOW

Sun-dried bricks kept houses in the Indus Valley cool. Natural plasters made of gypsum and bitumen were used. Cement that is used today must be manufactured, using energy.

Keeping the City Clean

The Indus Valley city planners were the first to make a system of drains. This maze of covered, sloping drains made sure water and dirt flowed away from the houses. This kept the cities clean and healthy.

The main drains were large. Cleaners could actually walk through to clean them. One brick with a notch cut in the center kept the drains clear.

Each house had a bath area. It included a bathing platform to stand on. The used water flowed into drains.

People threw their garbage in brick pits. From there it was taken away. The Indus Valley cities stayed clean.

Most houses were about the same size. However, some important people lived in large houses. Every home could store water. Some two-story houses even had pipes made of baked earth, or terra-cotta, that led water into the drain below.

▶The people of the Indus Valley knew that water flowed from a higher to a lower level. They used this knowledge to water their fields and to drain dirty water out of their homes and cities. This was the first and most detailed drainage and sewage system in the world.

THEN and NOW

In a city, proper disposal of waste is important. This was understood well by the Indus Valley town planners. Many cities today struggle to dispose of all the waste people create.

The Art of Fine Living

The Indus Valley craftspeople made necklaces from terra-cotta beads. Others made jewelry from shells and ivory. They also used stones and metals such as silver and gold.

Jewelers made beads from carnelian, agate, amethyst, turquoise, and a pretty stone called *faience*.

Jewels from the past. How lovely!

That's a bead from a necklace. We loved to make pretty things for ourselves and our homes.

◀Potters made pots on their wheels. Then artisans painted the pots.

▲Jewelers were busy people. The Indus Valley people loved to wear jewelry.

▲Toys were made of natural materials like clay, slate, wood, and stone.

Craftspeople made pots that were used in the homes. They painted and molded statues. They loved fine living and made perfume bottles.

Carpenters made and decorated furniture. They made pretty toys for children.

THEN and NOW

Potter's wheels were run by a pedal. Today, large ceramic and pottery factories use a lot of energy. The chemical paints they use pollute the air and water.

Moving Around

The people of the Indus Valley Civilization learned to tame animals. People rode horses, camels, and donkeys. Oxen pulled heavy carts of grain from the farm to the granary.

The main city streets were made for cart use. They curved at the corners so cart wheels could turn easily. The carts followed basic traffic rules.

How did you move around? Did you have cars?

Oh, no. We only used natural means of transportation!

▶The dock at Lothal was 700 feet long. It was made up of about one million bricks. It was bigger than many modern docks.

Moving water is a clean and renewable source of energy. The people of the Indus Valley used it to sail their boats.

Where the river was close to the city, people sailed on boats.
The people were good sailors and skilled in making boats.

In Harappa, boats brought grain to the city. Lothal was the largest port town. It had a busy harbor. Boats were built and repaired there. Traders came and went, carrying goods to and fro.

The sailors traveled far and wide. They took grain and cotton. Then they brought back things they needed.

THEN and NOW

People of the Indus Valley tamed elephants. They also crafted items of ivory from elephant tusks. Today, trading ivory has been banned across the world.

18-19

Rites and Rituals

Why do most of your seals have animals?

We lived close to nature and loved animals and plants. We loved having them on seals, pottery, and jewelry.

Thousands of Indus Valley seals have animals on them. But not all seals show animals. One has a seated man surrounded by animals. It is now called *Pashupati Shiva*.

Hundreds of statues of women are believed to be those of the Mother Goddess. It is believed that she may have been worshiped in every home. This is why so many of her statues have been found.

GREEN GEM The people of the Indus Valley worshiped nature. They were grateful for what nature gave them.

The people of the Indus Valley first buried their dead. Some historians believe they later cremated, or burned, the dead. Then they buried the ashes in terra-cotta urns or pots.

Priests carried out rituals. The Great Bath at Mohenjo Daro suggests that bathing was probably a part of a religious ceremony. Animal sacrifices were probably another ritual.

▲The unicorn seal may have been used in worship.

▲This statue of the Priest King was found in an unusual house in Mohenjo Daro. The house was beautifully decorated with special bricks. A niche was carved in a wall. The statue was lying between the walls.

▼Religious processions went around the cities. People carried flags and poles.

THEN and NOW

The statue of the Priest King was found in Mohenjo Daro in 1927. It is made of white soapstone. It is now in the National Museum in Karachi, Pakistan.

Ancient Attire

The people of the Indus Valley loved to dress up. Most of their clothes were draped and not sewn. Women wore a short skirt with a belt. They probably did not cut their hair. Statues of women found at the site show their hair tied up in fancy styles. Some wore fan-shaped headdresses decorated with flowers and terra-cotta cones. Some women spread their hair over a frame tied to the head. Over the forehead, they wore tiaras.

Men tied their long hair into a bun held in place by a ribbon or headband. Often, the band was made of gold and had holes for ribbons. The ends of the headband fell down the back.

What a beautiful robe! Tell me about it.

Each design is decorated with three holes. These round designs in between two leaves were colored red.

▶Both men and women loved to wear jewelry. They wore necklaces, bracelets, and bangles. Round beads were made into necklaces. Long beads were worn around the waist.

Men also liked to wear ornaments such as necklaces with pendants.

Most men did not wear a headdress. They kept their long hair swept on top of the head or to the side. Some men cut their hair but still wore it long enough to be swept back. They also trimmed their beards and mustaches short.

The Priest King wore a headband of gold with a round ornament in the center.

▶The statue of the Dancing Girl shows that the Indus Valley women loved to wear a lot of jewelry.

▶Women of the Indus Valley tried different ways of looking good. They wore fancy hairstyles, ornaments, and makeup.

THEN and NOW

The people of the Indus Valley Civilization wore clothes of natural, biodegradable fiber. Today, we wear clothes that have synthetic threads that do not degrade easily.

22-23

Mathemagicians!

The Indus Valley people were good with mathematics! This knowledge helped their traders and sailors.

As buyers and sellers, they were one of the first to come up with standard weights. This means the weights were the same in all their cities.

They could measure length and tell time. They made scales to weigh very small amounts. They could add and divide. This helped them build such neat houses and cities. Each brick was made to measure. These ancient people even knew fractions, or the decimal system of numbering.

What else did you do besides grow crops, hunt, and trade? Did your children study like I do?

Many of us studied different things.

GREEN GEM In addition to mining metals, the Indus Valley people also knew how to mix metals and produce bronze from copper and tin.

The builders knew different shapes. Most wells were round, but the one near the Great Bath was oval.

Sailors could travel the seas because they had instruments to help them navigate. One instrument measured parts of the horizon.

Their engineers studied the waves and tides. This helped them know how to build a sturdy dock.

Indus Valley people wrote in the Indus script. Except for the numbers, no one has been able to read it until now. It is found on seals, pottery, and jewelry. Archaeologists are still waiting for someone to make sense of the thousands of signs that were written from right to left.

▶The knowledge of mathematics helped traders, sailors, and builders make exact measurements. They could measure as little as .07 inches. That's less than one-tenth of your fingernail!

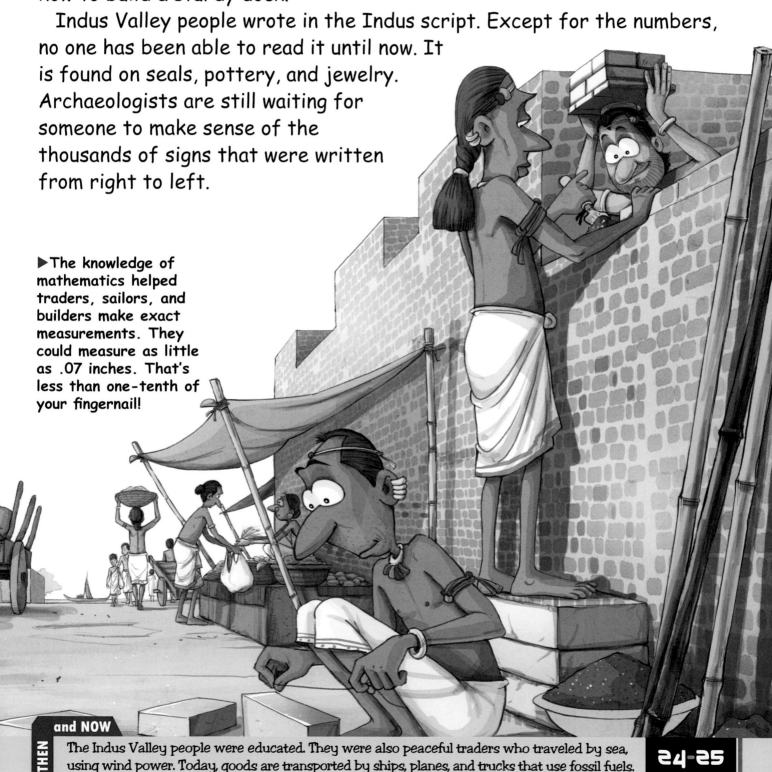

THEN and NOW

The Indus Valley people were educated. They were also peaceful traders who traveled by sea, using wind power. Today, goods are transported by ships, planes, and trucks that use fossil fuels.

24-25

Why Did They Disappear?

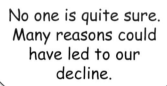

How could such a wonderful civilization end in ruins?

No one is quite sure. Many reasons could have led to our decline.

The Indus Valley was a great place to live, and the number of people kept growing. Having enough food became a problem.

The Indus River gave life to the civilization. But some believe it also ended the civilization. Floodwaters destroyed the cities time and again. Each time, the people tried to build a new city over the damaged one. Mohenjo Daro was rebuilt six times. Harappa was rebuilt five times.

▲Frequent floods damaged the cities. This could have finally caused the Indus Valley Civilization to die out.

GREEN GEM The Indus Valley Civilization is an important link to our past. So, it has been listed on UNESCO's World Heritage Site. Now no one can destroy the remains of these precious cities.

▼Some scientists believe that a terrible earthquake caused a water shortage.

When the first settlers moved in around 2600 B.C., the area was full of forests and animals. As the number of people grew, forests were cut. This slowly turned the place into a desert.

The climate also changed. It became drier and colder.

By 1900 B.C., the cities became difficult to live in. Even when people built new houses, it was hard to build drains over old ones. Food became a problem. Within the next hundred years, most people left the cities.

Some believe that Aryans came from far-off places and drove out the people who remained. Then they burned down parts of the city. The Indus Valley people were not prepared for these invaders. Their weapons, such as stone-tipped arrows, axes, bows and arrows, and daggers, were not enough.

THEN and NOW

When Mohenjo Daro was set up, it stood on a ridge. Over hundreds of years, the floods submerged the ridge.

Could this be the other half I am looking for?

Take it with you. Hand it over to a museum. They can repair it and keep it safe.

Green Lessons

- Rainwater harvesting was an important part of the Indus Valley Civilization.

- The well-planned cities of this civilization were incredibly clean. This was due to their well-maintained drainage system.

- Natural products such as mud and clay were used to make pottery and toys.

- Solar energy was used. Homes were built with sunbaked bricks.

- People of the Indus Valley used tools made of wood, stone, and metal.